The Ita Guide to Seeking Dual Citizenship as Blood Right

By Valerie Winkler

Table of Contents

Preface

Americans are able to keep their U.S. citizenship and obtain citizenship from a select number of other countries. Italy is one of them. If you are a direct descendant of an Italian then you may be eligible to apply for citizenship via jure sanguinis, which is Latin for "right of blood". You can verify whether you are eligible in Chapter 4 – Eligibility.

I hope this guide gives you the answers you are looking for. If not, check out my website at http://italianamericandualcitizenship.com or send me an email at mailto:Valerie@italianamericandualcitizenship.com and I'll be sure to add in more details to the next version of my book.

Chapter 1: Benefits of Dual Citizenship

People have many different reasons for wanting to obtain dual citizenship. Since you selected this book, you likely already have some of your own reasons. It can be a lengthy and costly process to have your Italian citizenship recognized so you should think about your goals for obtaining citizenship and whether it's worth it before you embark on this journey. In this chapter, I've shared some of the benefits of dual citizenship.

The right to work overseas

Some Americans may find that their job prospects are better overseas or have just always wanted the option to be able to work or create a business outside of the United States. As an Italian citizen, you will not only obtain rights to work, vote and own property in Italy, you will also be eligible to work throughout the European Union.

Many large global employers may be willing to sponsor a work visa for Americans to work overseas on a short-term assignment. However, the process takes some time and has costs associated for the employer. As an Italian citizen, you may have a leg up on your coworkers vying for that opportunity since a work visa will not be required for you to work in those countries (saving the company money) and you can leave more quickly for an immediate need versus someone requiring a work visa where they need to allow time for processing.

As a dual American/Italian citizen you can work in any of the 27 European Union member states and the 4 European Free Trade Association (EFTA) member states, in addition to the United States.

Here is a listing of the 27 member states of the European Union.

1. Austria

2. Belgium

3. Bulgaria

4. Cyprus

5. Czech Republic

6. Denmark

7. Estonia

8. Finland

9. France

10. Germany

11. Greece

12. Hungary

13. Ireland

14. Italy

15. Latvia

16. Lithuania

17. Luxembourg

18. Malta

19. Netherlands

20. Poland

21. Portugal

22. Romania

23. Slovakia

24. Slovenia

25. Spain

26. Sweden

27. United Kingdom

The 4 EFTA member states are Iceland, Liechtenstein, Norway and Switzerland. Some portions of Norway may be more restrictive as it relates to the laws related to the freedom of moving persons. You should always review the specific rules and requirements for each country you are interesting in living or working in and not rely solely on the information presented here.

You may also find it easier to obtain work visas for other countries where you may be interested in applying. Each country has different rules for obtaining work visas so you should always check the rules for both USA and Italy to see which is more generous.

The right to vote in Italy

If you want to have a voice in elections, obtaining Italian citizenship will grant you the right to vote in Italy. Once you obtain citizenship, make sure you keep your local consulate up to date with your address and inform them of your interest to absentee vote.

The right to own property overseas

Many countries require that you are a citizen in order to be able to own property. As an Italian citizen you will be eligible to buy property in Italy and some other European Union countries.

Ease of travelling

If you frequently travel overseas, you will find it much easier and faster to travel specifically when entering or travelling between European Union countries using your Italian passport. Have you seen the EU lane in major airports in the European Union? It's significantly faster which is very helpful when you have a connecting flight. Additionally, similar to the work visa, there are different rules for each country when obtaining travel visas. If you want to travel to a country outside the US and European Union, you should always check the travel visa rules for both US and Italy to determine which is easier or less expensive to obtain. For example, in 2013, you can obtain an e-visitor visa to visit Australia for 90 days at no cost whereas the cheapest option for an U.S. Citizen is to go with the Electronic Travel Authority (ETA) which carries an AUD20 service fee.

Access to a wider range of financial opportunities

As an Italian citizen, you are eligible to invest in offshore mutual funds and securities that you would not otherwise be eligible to invest in as solely a U.S. citizen.

Free public health care

If you wish to move to Italy, you can take advantage of the free public healthcare offered by the country. Having dual citizenship is an excellent insurance policy overall since you will now have multiple options if anything changes significantly in one country or the other. For health care specifically, let's say you end up with a terminal disease and the costs start to become unbearable for you and your family. Now you have the option to alleviate some of that pressure by moving to another country that will provide you the necessary care without that expense. Certainly you'd need to weigh other factors, but having dual citizenship gives you this option.

Attend tuition-free universities

Perhaps you'd like to take advantage of the free university education available in a country in the European Union. This may be a great option for you or your children as an alternative to the expensive American universities while getting some cultural perspective overseas. Please research the individual universities by going to their website for requirements. There are some taxes involved and some universities can charge more based on recent laws but the tuition portion of a college expense is cheaper than a U.S. education. This does not include room and board or food, so you'll have to compare these expenses based on your current cost of living. Some universities may also require that you meet specific residency requirements to take advantage of the cheaper European Union rate.

Sentimental reasons

Some people have no interest in moving, working or travelling overseas but simply want to obtain citizenship for sentimental reasons. Obtaining dual citizenship via jure sanguinis (blood right) is your birthright so whatever your reason or reasons are it does not matter for purposes of your application.

Chapter 2: Things to Consider

You've read about the benefits but what are some of the cons in obtaining dual citizenship?

Just like people have varied reasons for wanting dual citizenship, there are many reasons why people may be apprehensive in moving forward with their application. By and large, if you intend to continue living in the United States there should not be any negative impacts related to your dual citizenship status. I am not a lawyer or tax consultant, so you will want to check with professionals for any of your specific concerns.

Lengthy Process

As I mentioned before, this is a lengthy process. Many consulates currently have a 15 month wait time to get an appointment. Assuming you are well prepared for this appointment, it could easily take another 6 months to get the confirmation of your citizenship recognition back from Italy after that. With this book, I try to help you be overly prepared for that visit so that you can get your citizenship recognized in the shortest time possible. I don't want you to be like the many people on citizenship forums who say it took 3-5 years. My total process from scheduling an appointment to receiving my letter showing citizenship took 16 months, so it is possible to obtain more quickly. (And that was with a 15 month wait for the appointment.)

Costly Process

Beginning July 8, 2014, the consulates are now charging 300 Euros as an application fee, regardless of outcome. This has been updated on the major consulate websites (i.e. Miami, New York), some of the smaller consulates have not updated their website at time of this writing but I expect that they are all charging this fee and have just not updated the information yet. Prior to that, there was no fee to the consulate to have your Italian citizenship recognized. However, in order to prove that you are a direct blood descendant and eligible for citizenship you must obtain and provide original documents to the consulate which can quickly become costly. Your cost will vary based on the following factors.

- Total number of documents you need (more documents, more money)

- State or county you need the document from (each state/county has different fees)

- Whether you engage professional help to search for documents or information related to your ancestors

- How many copies you want (more copies, more money)

- Whether you need to travel in order to obtain documents

- Total number of documents requiring corrections (you will need to pay both for the correction and for a new copy of the document)

- Total number of documents requiring translation

- Total number of documents requiring apostille

- Total number of documents requiring a letter of exemplification (NYC records)

It will also cost you a lot of your precious time to track down the records, especially if any require a correction. The total number of documents you need is largely based on how many generations you need to go back to reach your ancestor born in Italy. If your parent was born in Italy than you have much less documentation needed than say if you are going back to your great-grandparent.

I've listed some general costs below to help give you an idea of your final cost. Some have wide variations so this may not be representative of your final cost.

- Phone call to book an appointment (they charge by the minute) ~$10

- Ancestry.com subscription (if you need this resource to help in your research) ~$19.99 to $44.99 per month

- Obtain National Archives records (naturalization paperwork) ~$7 to $25 per record

- Obtain Social Security records (to obtain pertinent information you may need for other records) ~$27 per record

- United States Citizenship and Immigration Services (USCIS) records (naturalization paperwork) ~$20 per record

- Translations ~$30 per page (if heavy text, ~$60 per page)

- Birth, marriage, death certificates ~$15 - $120 per certificate (largely dependent on county, whether you are picking up in person or shipping)

- Apostilles ~$5 to $25 per apostille

- Corrections to certificates ~$15-25 (cost of correction only, does not include cost of a new certificate containing correction)

Taxes

If you live and work in the United States, you will not owe taxes to Italy. I am not a tax advisor so you will of course want to validate everything with your own tax attorney. If you do work overseas, you will need to file in both countries and should obtain a tax attorney to ensure that you file correctly.

Military obligations

Laws change frequently so you will want to validate with a lawyer, however per the San Francisco consulate, if you are a male under the age of forty-five you will have military obligations to Italy. The military obligation can generally be fulfilled by completing some paperwork in the pertinent Consulate, after your citizenship has been processed. However, if you are under the age of twenty seven, until you reach that age you may not permanently reside in Italy for reasons other than study, unless you wish to serve in the Italian Armed Forces. Further information on military obligations can be obtained by contacting the military section of the pertinent Italian Consulate or Embassy, depending on where you are residing.

Jobs

If you plan to work in certain government jobs, having dual citizenship could hurt you. This is true for jobs where your loyalties could be questioned due to serving two masters including security related government jobs.

Laws

You are required to follow the laws of both countries in which you are a citizen.

It is also worth noting that when you travel you will need to decide which passport to use. You should always use your U.S. passport when entering or exiting the U.S. and you should use your Italian passport when entering or exiting Italy. When visiting other countries, the passport you use will determine which Embassy will protect you should you run into any problems.

Chapter 3: Checklist

1. Verify eligibility (or when naturalization is not completely known, your likelihood of eligibility)

2. Call to make an appointment with your local consulate

3. Create a comprehensive list of documents needed for application

4. Collect documentation

5. Discuss with family members

6. Verify documentation

7. Correct documentation, if applicable

8. Prepare for appointment

9. Create list of discrepancies, if applicable

10. Attend appointment

11. Receive recognition of citizenship

12. Apply for passport, if desired

Chapter 4: Eligibility

In order to gain Italian citizenship via jure sanguinis (right of blood), you must have an Italian ancestor in your bloodline.

Tracing the Blood Line

The concept here is that you must look back to your closest blood relative born in Italy and trace the path from that person down to you. If you have Italian blood relatives on your maternal (mother) and paternal (father) side, it's generally easier to qualify following your father's line. This is due to a law that did not allow a woman to transfer her Italian citizenship to children prior to January 1, 1948. If you are eligible following either blood line, than just choose the one that you prefer which is likely the one that will be easier to obtain documentation. Generally, this will be the line that contains the most living relatives in the path.

It's helpful to write down the path you will follow by starting with your closest blood relative born in Italy along with birth dates and locations, if you have them available.

Pietro (Italy)
|
Leonardo (New York, 1918)
|
Angelo (New Jersey, 1940)
|
Rosa (New Jersey, 1964)

Reviewing for eligibility - The Female Factor

Is there a female on your list? If so, the female was not eligible to pass the Italian citizenship to her child if the child was born before January 1, 1948. Let's look at two examples.

Example 1 (Ineligibility)

Gioacchino (male) was born in Italy. He had a child, Rosina (female), born in the United States in 1915. Rosina had a child, Rosa, born in the United States in 1940. Rosa is not eligible for dual citizenship via jure sanguinis following her mother's line since

Rosa was born before January 1, 1948. Her mother, Rosina, was not eligible to pass her Italian citizenship to her child.

Example 2 (Eligibility)

Gioacchino (male) was born in Italy. He had a child, Rosina (female), born in the United States in 1925. Rosina had a child, Rosa, born in the United States in 1950. Rosa is eligible for dual citizenship via jure sanguinis following her mother's line since Rosa was born after January 1, 1948. Her mother, Rosina, was eligible to gain Italian citizenship from her father (assuming he did not give up that right before her birth). As an Italian citizen through blood, Rosina was then eligible to pass that blood right to her children born after January 1, 1948.

Reviewing for eligibility - Renounced Citizenship

You must determine if anyone renounced Italian citizenship in your line. Sometimes Italian citizenship can be renounced when the Italian citizen applied for U.S. citizenship. If you do not know the answer to this question yet, you will figure it out as you begin your research to prepare the paperwork required for your dual citizenship application.

You will also need to determine whether anyone naturalized before 1912. If so, you are not eligible. (Law n. 555 of June 13, 1912).

Another important factor is whether U.S. citizenship was acquired via naturalization before the birth of your direct descendant.

Example 1 (Ineligibility)

Pietro was born in Italy in 1880 and moved to the United States in 1900. Pietro naturalized in 1914 and then gave birth to Leonardo in 1915. Leonardo gave birth to a son, Angelo, in 1935. Angelo gave birth to a daughter, Rosa, in 1955. Because Pietro naturalized in 1914 before his son Leonardo was born, he was not eligible to transfer his Italian citizenship to Leonardo. Therefore, none of Leonardo's descendants are eligible for Italian citizenship via jure sanguinis.

Example 2 (Eligibility)

Pietro, from example 1 above, also gave birth to a son, Gioacchino, in 1913. Gioacchino is eligible for Italian citizenship because he was born before Pietro naturalized. Assuming Gioacchino never renounced his citizenship, he was eligible to pass his blood right down to his descendants. This is an example where cousins following a path from the same person (Pietro) may be eligible for dual citizenship while others are not, depending on the birth order and timing of naturalization.

A good way to verify the timing of this is to either acquire that naturalization paperwork through United States Citizenship and Immigration Services or to review the census files containing important information about the status of citizenship. There is a question on the census file "Naturalized or Alien" that will give you a clue into the status of your ancestor's citizenship. If you see "AL" listed that means "Alien" and your ancestor had not yet naturalized. If you see "PA" listed that means "First Papers" indicating that your ancestor had started the process to apply but was not yet naturalized.

Here is a sample of this section from the 1920 census file.

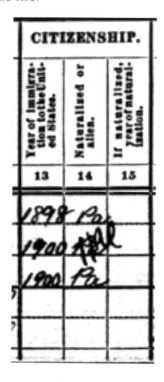

Chapter 5: Getting Started

Step 1: Make an appointment with your closest Italian consulate. This is the first step because most consulates will not be able to fit you in for another year or longer. Once you have your appointment date in hand, you can spend the 12-18 month wait collecting the necessary documentation for your application.

There are 11 main Italian consulates in the US; Boston, Chicago, Detroit, Houston, Los Angeles, Miami, Newark, New York, Philadelphia, San Francisco, and Washington D.C.

First find your state below to determine which consulate services your state.

1. Alabama - Miami

2. Alaska - San Francisco

3. Arizona - Los Angeles

4. Arkansas - Houston

5. California

   a. Southern California (Counties of San Luis Obispo, Kern, San Bernardino, Santa Barbara, Ventura, Los Angeles, Riverside, San Diego, Imperial Valley, Orange) - Los Angeles

   b. All other counties - San Francisco

6. Colorado - Chicago

7. Connecticut - New York

8. Delaware - Philadelphia

9. Florida - Miami

10. Georgia - Miami

11. Hawai'i - San Francisco

12. Idaho - San Francisco

13. Illinois - Chicago

14. Indiana - Detroit

15. Iowa - Chicago

16. Kansas - Chicago

17. Kentucky - Detroit

18. Louisiana - Houston

19. Maine - Boston

20. Maryland

    a. Montgomery and Prince George counties - Washington, D.C.

    b. All other counties - Philadelphia

21. Massachusetts - Boston

22. Michigan - Detroit

23. Minnesota - Chicago

24. Mississippi - Miami

25. Missouri - Chicago

26. Montana - San Francisco

27. Nebraska - Chicago

28. Nevada - Los Angeles

29. New Hampshire - Boston

30. New Jersey

    a. Atlantic, Burlington, Camden, Cape May, Cumberland, Gloucester, Ocean and Salem counties - Philadelphia

    b. Bergen, Essex, Hudson, Hunterdon, Mercer, Middlesex, Monmouth, Morris, Passaic, Somerset, Sussex, Union, Warren counties - Newark

    c. All other counties - New York

31. New Mexico - Los Angeles

32. New York - New York

33. North Carolina - Philadelphia

34. North Dakota - Chicago

35. Ohio - Detroit

36. Oklahoma - Houston

37. Oregon - San Francisco

38. Pennsylvania - Philadelphia

39. Rhode Island - Boston

40. South Carolina - Miami

41. South Dakota - Chicago

42. Tennessee - Detroit

43. Texas - Houston

44. Utah - San Francisco

45. Vermont - Boston

46. Virginia

   a. Arlington and Fairfax counties - Washington, D.C.

   b. All other counties - Philadelphia

47. Washington - San Francisco

48. West Virginia - Philadelphia

49. Wisconsin - Chicago

50. Wyoming - Chicago

Other locations served by the consulates:

1. Puerto Rico - Miami

2. American Virgin Islands - Miami

3. British Virgin Islands - Miami

4. Caymans - Miami

5. The Dutch Islands of St. Maarten - Miami

6. St. Eustatius and Saba - Miami

7. Turks and Caicos - Miami

8. Bahamas - Miami

9. British Territories of Bermuda Islands - New York

10. Guam - San Francisco

11. Northern Mariana Islands - San Francisco

12. Samoa - San Francisco

13. Wake Island - San Francisco

14. Midways Islands - San Francisco

15. Johnston Atoll - San Francisco

See the Directory of Consulates in this guide for the website and contact information of your consulate. Once you go to the website, you can select which language (English or Italian) you want to use to view the site. There is a navigation banner at the top of the page, select Consular Services from that menu and then you will be able to select "Citizenship" to see the rules and instructions outlined by your consulate. Tip: Google Chrome is a great browser to download for your research as it will automatically translate web pages in other languages for you.

Los Angeles, Miami and New York utilize a service by Abtran to schedule appointments for dual citizenship applications. There is a per minute charge for this service but it is the only way you can make an appointment. At time of publishing, the number was 900-446-2244 for charges to appear on your phone statement or 800-686-4446 for charges to appear on your credit card statement at a rate of $2.49 per minute.

Newark and Philadelphia utilize a similar service by ISP Italy to schedule their appointments for dual citizenship applications. The number is 800-531-0840.

Chapter 6: Checking in with Family Members

It's a good idea to check in with all your family members (parents, grandparents, sisters, brothers, aunts, uncles, cousins) to let them know that you are embarking on the journey to dual citizenship and find out whether any of them are interested, or perhaps applied previously. Not only can they potentially help you obtain the documentation you need for the application, they may also be able to share in the expense of obtaining the documentation if they are also interested in applying.

Previously, when someone applied to have their citizenship recognized at a consulate, a file was created and stored at the consulate for that family. By knowing whether a family file exists and what is already in it, you could have saved time and expense by not having to acquire any shared documents. For example, if you and your cousin both want to apply you could have shared documents for your grandparent's birth and marriage certificates. Unfortunately, sometime in 2013, the consulates stopped being open to this concept. They are now requiring that each applicant provide all the required documentation. However, it is still a good idea to identify who else in your family is interested because you will still save some money when ordering multiple copies of the same document.

Parents & Grandparents

If anyone in the direct line that you are following to obtain your citizenship is interested in applying, e.g. your mother or father, and you live in the same consulate jurisdiction, you should share your appointment with them and have it recognized at the same time. It is worth noting that even though they are higher in the bloodline than you are and that they have to be eligible to have their Italian citizenship recognized in order for you to gain your citizenship, they do not receive it automatically by your citizenship being recognized. This process is to ensure that the family member wants to have their Italian citizenship formally recognized as well.

Siblings

Your brothers and sisters will need all the same documents as you to obtain citizenship minus their personal documents (birth certificate, marriage certificate if applicable) so there is definite value in teaming up with a sibling for obtaining citizenship.

Spouse

Since this is a guide for Americans who wish to obtain dual citizenship, I have also made the assumption that you live in America. If you have been married at least 3 years (or 1.5 years if you have children with your spouse), your spouse is eligible to apply for dual citizenship as a person married to an Italian citizen. If this applies to you and your spouse wishes to become an Italian citizen, you should schedule an appointment for your spouse to take place about 6 months to a year after your appointment. This will ensure that your paperwork has been sent over to Italy and you have received back formal acknowledgement of your recognition before your spouse's appointment. The appointment for your spouse is separate from your appointment and your appointment must take place before your spouse's since you have to first be recognized as a citizen before your spouse can try to obtain citizenship through marriage. You must supply your marriage certificate and spousal information at your appointment to ensure that you marriage is already registered at the Commune in Italy and that you are registered at the Consulate as an Italian Citizen Residing Abroad (A.I.R.E.). There are of course other ways for folks to obtain dual citizenship and different rules if you already live in Italy. This book is not intended to go into all that detail but you will find all the information you need by checking out your consulate's website.

Children

If you have natural born children that are under the age of 18 at the time of your appointment, you can supply their birth certificates to have them recognized as dual citizens. If your children are over the age of 18, they must apply separately but can share your appointment.

As always, check the rules on your consulate's website because they are known to change. If you have any specific questions that aren't covered by the website details (you will), email the consulate. They usually respond very quickly.

Chapter 7: Getting Started on Collecting Documents

First, let me orient you to the types of documents you will need and then you can follow my tips for ordering.

Birth Certificates – Birth certificates will be necessary for everyone in your bloodline starting from the ancestor born in Italy down to any children you have. You should also obtain birth certificates for the spouses of anyone in your bloodline. These folks will be referred to as part of the "non-Italian" line on the consulate website and throughout this book. In reality, these folks may also be Italian as well but it is a way to distinguish that they are part of the line that you are not following. Birth certificates must be in "long form". There are many versions of birth certificates out there and different ways you may have obtained yours originally, i.e. hospital, county, state. The consulate requires the long form version of the certificate containing more details regarding the parents and child than you would see on a "short form". In most cases, you will need to order a new copy of any birth certificates you may already have since most folks either have only 1 original or have a short form version. Since you will be giving your original birth certificates to the consulate, you will likely want to retain an original for your own records anyway. You will not get back any of the originals that the consulate takes for your file.

Marriage Certificates - Marriage certificates are also necessary for everyone in your bloodline starting from the ancestor born in Italy down to yours, if applicable. Marriage certificates must be in "long form". Just like birth certificates, there are many versions of marriage certificates out there and different ways you may have obtained yours originally, i.e. church, county, state. The consulate requires the long form version of the certificate containing more details regarding the bride and groom than you would see on a "short form". In most cases, you will need to order a new copy of any marriage certificates you may already have since most folks either have only 1 original or have a short form version. Since you will be giving your original marriage certificates to the consulate, you will likely want to retain an original for your own records.

Death Certificates - Death certificates are also necessary for everyone in your bloodline starting from the ancestor born in Italy, as applicable. Death certificates must be in "long form" but do not require the cause of death. This is noteworthy as some counties or states will charge extra or require additional proof of your relationship to the deceased if you want to have the cause of death displayed on the certificate.

Apostilles – The consulate will require an apostille for all the birth, marriage and death certificates in your Italian line. You should also obtain the apostille for the certificates on your "non-Italian" line, in case they are required. An apostille is similar to when you get something notarized, but in this case the notary is the issuing state of the certificate. The physical apostille is an additional piece of paper that is affixed to the certificate to certify that the document is real and accurate for the country you specify, in this case Italy. When requesting an apostille, you always need to specify the country for which you need the apostille.

Certificate of Naturalization or Statement of No Record – This is a certificate showing the date and information related to the naturalization of your ancestor. If your ancestor never naturalized, then you will need to obtain a letter stating that the National Archives and Records Administration (NARA) and United States Citizenship and Immigration Services (USCIS) completed a search and found no record.

Letter of Exemplification – If you need to obtain any birth, marriage or death certificates from New York City, you will need to obtain a letter of exemplification from the county clerk before you can obtain an apostille. This is a specific requirement that the state of New York imposes for any records coming from the city of New York.

Translations – You will need to have all your U.S. birth, marriage and death certificates translated to Italian for the documents from your Italian line. You should also have the documents from your non-Italian bloodline translated just in case. You do not need to have any documents from Italy translated to English for purposes of your application, though you may wish to do so for your family genealogy purposes. You also do not need to have the apostilles, Certificate of Naturalization, Statement of No Record or Letter of Exemplification translated.

If you are unsure of whether you qualify because you have not yet validated if your ancestor renounced Italian citizenship, then try to obtain the Certificate of Naturalization or Statement of No

Record and any certificates from Italy first. These will likely take you the longest to research and obtain so you can hold off on getting your United States certificates until you are certain that you will qualify. I make this recommendation only to save you the expense and time of getting all your other documents if you don't really need them. This can be a very costly process as I outlined in a prior chapter. If this is not a concern for you, then go ahead and start ordering all your documents right away. If you don't already have these certificates, there is a lot of information you may learn that you didn't already know. Since I was doing all this research anyway, I took this time to become the family genealogist and build out our family tree, interviewing family members and learning more about our history for both my Italian and "non-Italian" side as well as my spouse's family history.

Tips for ordering United States birth, marriage and death certificates:

1. Create a comprehensive list of all the certificates you need to order including the state and county where the event took place. Refer to the Toolkit at the end of the book for a sample spreadsheet to do this.

2. Find out the apostille process for the state where the certificate was issued. While you will order most certificates via the VitalChek website and select "Apostille" or "Dual Citizenship" to ensure you receive the right version (long form) of the certificate, some states have a multi-step process for obtaining the apostille and some will provide the appropriate version of the certificate and apostille at once. This can also save you some money if you have multiple

certificates in the same state but not the same county.

3. Before ordering certificates on VitalChek make sure you have a comprehensive list of all the certificates you need to order by state and county (from step 1). This will allow you to order the certificates from the same state at the same time often saving you some money because you will only have to pay one shipping fee. A lot of states and counties require that you have it mailed via UPS and the shipping fee can range from $17-$47 just for that piece of the order. Because of this, I also recommend that you order multiple copies. You will typically only pay one shipping and one processing fee for copies of the same certificate. Duplicate certificates are usually cheaper than the cost of the first so for a few dollars more you can have the security of knowing that you have a back-up in case one of your documents gets lost in the mail while obtaining an apostille, etc.

4. Make sure to read the rules regarding who may obtain the certificate before you order. For example, if your grandparents are still living it will be easier if you have them obtain their own certificates. This is another example where each state (and sometimes county) has different rules on who may obtain the document.

5. Create and maintain a spreadsheet with the detailed list of all the documents you need to acquire. Document when you requested the certificate and from whom. This will help you determine when you need to follow-up, if a few months have gone by and you have not yet received your documentation.

Make sure you start early on obtaining

documents. Just because you know you have 15+ months doesn't mean you should wait. Besides the fact that it can take some time to research and order the documents, once you get the documents you will still need to have them translated, obtain your apostilles, and in some cases have the documents corrected if you notice any name variances. It is this last point that could cause you a lot of last minute running around to find out how to get the name corrected. In fact, the name discrepancy may also cause you trouble in obtaining the certificate in the first place.

While talking to your family members or researching your genealogy, you should obtain as many records related to your family as possible even if they are not specifically required for your application. In many cases, these documents will give you clues to help you obtain the required documentation. In other cases, the consulate or state vital records office may require those documents as additional proof when trying to obtain records or corrections of records because they substantiate your lineage to the person and therefore your authority to request documents or corrections, or it proves the name or age discrepancy of that ancestor. Some of the documents that can be used as further proof are baptismal certificates, passport applications, copies of driver's licenses and social security applications.

While you are doing your research, you should keep copies of anything relevant that substantiates birth dates, birth places, marriage dates, marriage places, status of naturalization, et cetera. In the event that there is a discrepancy between the dates on certain documents, this will provide you added proof of your ancestor's history. It is very common for there to be discrepancies in names, dates and ages between varying documents. Sometimes this is due to typographical errors or language barriers; in other cases, your ancestor may have fudged the date a little for varied reasons.

Naturalization/Statement of No Record

Census records are a great place to get important information about your ancestor. The census will list the names of your ancestors, what country they came from, and (for most years) the status of their naturalization. This is excellent proof for the naturalization paperwork you will need to provide with your application.

You should be aware that there are many misspellings in census records so it may be difficult to find your ancestor due to misspelled first or last names. Additionally, since your ancestor may not have spoken English many times ages were guesstimates from the census taker or provided by the children who could speak English and are, therefore, not always correct. You can also find out when your ancestor first came to America on these records but this is also sometimes based on recollection and not always accurate once you find the ship records.

If you determine that your ancestor never naturalized, you will need to obtain a letter from both the National Archives and Records Administration (NARA) and the United States Citizenship and Immigration Services (USCIS).

Requesting a search/letter from USCIS

You can submit a request for a genealogy search from USCIS by going to the website: http://www.uscis.gov/portal/site/uscis and selecting "Genealogy" from the Services menu on the left. There is a $20 fee to do an Index Search. Follow the instructions on the page. There is an option to complete the request online.

If it is determined that there your ancestor did not naturalize due to no record found, then you will need an official "no record" letter from USCIS. At last check, they detail the process on their website in the following section: Home>Genealogy>Genealogy Frequently Asked Questions>Dual Citizenship Research FAQS.

Here is an excerpt:

"How can the USCIS Genealogy Program help me locate documents to support a foreign application for dual citizenship?

A Genealogy Index Search Request can provide you with information about a naturalization record found, or the failure to locate any naturalization for a given subject. A "no record" response does not serve as a certification of nonexistence (see below).

How do I get certification of non-existence of a record?

A "no record" letter from the Genealogy Program can be forwarded along with your request to the USCIS Records Services Branch for an agency decision to issue a certificate of non-existence.

You may also write directly to the Records Services Branch, but it is important all such letters contain information to specifically identify the immigrant. For example, requests must contain the immigrant's name (including all variants and aliases), date of birth, place of birth, and as much information as possible about when and where the immigrant arrived in or lived in the United States. Names of immediate immigrant relatives can also be helpful.

In all cases the immigrant must be deceased. If the immigrant's birth date is less than 100 years before the request date, requests for certification of non-existence must include a copy of the immigrant's death certificate.

Requests for this service should be addressed to: U.S. Citizenship and Immigration Services, ATTN: Records Operations Branch, 1200 First Street NE, Washington, D.C. 20529-2204.

Can the USCIS Genealogy Program provide a copy or a certified copy of naturalization records?

A Genealogy Record Request can provide an information copy of a naturalization record. The Genealogy Program does not provide certified copies.

If you need only a copy of the naturalization certificate (not certified) to satisfy requirements for your foreign application for dual citizenship, you may submit a G-1041A Record Request for the naturalization certificate only. Doing so can eliminate any additional processing delay resulting from information about the immigrant's children that may need review under the Privacy Act. To request only the *certificate, write "Dual Citz-Natz Certificate Only" on your request from G-1041A or in the "optional information section" of your online request."*

Requesting a search/letter from NARA

In order to determine whether the NARA has a copy of your ancestor's naturalization paperwork, you will want to go to http://www.archives.gov/research/naturalization/. There will be links based on the state in which you would have expected your ancestor to naturalize. In the event that you do not believe your ancestor ever applied for American citizenship, you will need to obtain a Statement of No Record. You can do this by reaching out to the county or state where your ancestor lived and request a review of the records on your behalf by someone in the NARA. If they can't find any record researching applicable years and all name variations, then they will supply you with a statement of no record.

See the sample email in the appendix "Sample Letters" section for an email that you can provide to NARA to get your statement of no record if it is determined that your ancestor did not naturalize. They did not charge a fee for this.

New York City Birth and Death Records

New York City vital records require a letter of exemplification, in addition to the apostille. The letter of exemplification must be obtained by the county clerk and supplied with the birth or death record when you submit request for apostille.

Las Vegas Marriage Certificates

If one of the marriage certificates you need to obtain is from Las Vegas, you will also need to obtain the marriage license from Clark County. This is due to the fact that there is limited personal information on the actual marriage certificate and the Affidavit of Application for Marriage License contains considerable more information that the consulate needs to substantiate the marriage. In 2012, the fee for obtaining the Affidavit of Application for Marriage License was $7 USD and could not be ordered via the County Clerk website. I've included a sample letter that you can send to County Clerk along with a money order or bank cashier check in the Sample Letters section.

Florida Certificates

If you need to order birth, marriage or death certificates for events that took place in Florida, do not use the VitalChek website. Fill out the applicable form and follow the instructions on the following website:
http://www.doh.state.fl.us/planning_eval/vital_statistics/apostille.htm

This option is faster and cheaper and ensures you have the long form version obtained from Jacksonville that will be required from Tallahassee to give you the apostille.

Iowa apostilles

Iowa will allow you to request the apostille via fax so long as you have obtained the record and can provide the documentation as part of the fax request. They will then send you the apostille in the mail and you can affix it to your vital record. The fee was only $5 in 2011 and you can pay via credit card.

Resources

Ancestry.com is a great resource for obtaining census records and finding dates and locations of events you weren't able to obtain from family members. The more information you already know and adding best guesses to locations and dates will make your search a little easier. You may even find long lost cousins who have started building their family trees that includes your common ancestors!

EllisIsland.org is another great resource for obtaining information about when your ancestor first came to America.

Chapter 8: What to expect at your consulate appointment

Because you are applying via jure sanguinis, there will be no hard questions asked at your appointment. Acquiring Italian citizenship is your birthright so the approval (or denial) is solely based on whether you are able to prove the bloodline exists. You do not need to provide any reason for why you want the citizenship recognized or what your intentions are (i.e. travel, move) once it's acquired. I was not even asked anything of the sort at my appointment because it's irrelevant.

The appointment will go something like this...

1. Consulate rep will ask you to first provide him or her with the birth record of the person born in Italy that is your ancestor. He or she will review it and write down some key information.

2. Then the rep will ask you to provide the marriage certificate for that same person. He or she will review it and make sure the names match and the age and birth dates match up to substantiate that it is one and the same person.

3. This will continue until you get down to your personal records (birth & marriage, if applicable).

Each time, the rep will be checking dates, ages and names to make sure that everything substantiates that the same people are referenced throughout. They will also make sure you have originals, apostilles and translations when needed.

It is very important that you have all your paperwork ready to go, easy to find and you've checked all the dates and spellings of names to make sure they match up before you go to your appointment so you can have records corrected, if needed.

I brought along all the information from my research including apostilles and translations for the "non-Italian" bloodline just in case. In the end, they only needed a small portion of what I'd prepared but they also ended up taking some information that I didn't expect them to want, like the census records showing the other children of my ancestor which was also further proof that my ancestor did not naturalize since there is a question in the census to that affect.

I've spoken with many others getting dual citizenship at various consulates and all have been lenient in not requiring a brand new appointment (with 15 month wait time) if you are missing one or two documents. Instead, they create your file at the first meeting and allow you to mail in the remaining documents. Because of this, I suggest that you do not miss your appointment even if you think you might be missing something. Having said that, you should try to have everything ready for that appointment otherwise you will have a much longer wait for them to process your trailing documentation.

While not needed for my citizenship, I had to provide additional proof to get my marriage on record at my Italian commune. It took well over 6 months and multiple follow-ups for status before I got confirmation that it had been forwarded to my commune in Italy. I also found out that if you got married in the jurisdiction of a different consulate than the one you currently reside, the marriage certificate first goes through that consulate for verification before being forwarded on to your Italian commune. This is important information to know if your spouse intends to obtain dual citizenship via marriage once yours is recognized. You will need to make sure that your Italian commune records the details of your marriage certificate in advance of your spouse's application and that you obtain a record of their transcription.

Chapter 9: Preparing for your consulate appointment

The consulate will be reviewing all the documentation you've been collecting to identify any discrepancies between names and dates. Do this in advance of your appointment and attempt to correct any discrepancies to make sure your appointment goes smoothly.

You should create a list of all documents you need and verify that the names are consistent with the correct spelling for both first and last names. If birth dates appear on multiple documents for the same person, verify that all birth dates and ages listed match.

What if they don't match?

You need to request a record correction from the issuing state or county. You will need to provide proof to justify the correction you are requesting. This process can take many months (or years), which is why you want to do this check and make the request as early as possible. All consulates are a little different with the types of discrepancies they are willing to forgive so you should be on the safe side and make the request for all discrepancies. Bring proof that you've made the correction request with you to the appointment if you have not yet received the corrected document. It is worth noting that when you make a correction to a vital record, the correction along with the person who requested it is attached to the original record.

What is proof that I made a correction request?

You will have to submit an application for correction, so make a photocopy of this at the very least. Some county and state vital records departments will also issue you a letter indicating that you have made the correction request.

Modifying Records

Check the website for the state in which you need to have a record corrected. Most states have a template correction form that must be used to make the correction.

If you have the luxury of doing this in person, you can usually expedite the request. Additionally, if the local city or township can make corrections they are sometimes faster than making the request at the state level. If you go in person, try to get a contact name, phone number and email address so you can check on the status of your request.

First Name Discrepancies

You will often find that there are first name discrepancies related to nicknames or Anglicization. For example, Pietro may become Peter or Pete. Some consulates will forgive this as it is commonly recognized to be the same name; others may not depending on how obvious the translation is. New York is a stickler for exact names. I had trouble obtaining my grandmother's birth certificate because her name on her birth certificate is listed as "Antonina" but all other documents (marriage, social security, etc.) are listed as "Anne". Their argument was that this might not be one in the same person even though I had a short form version of her birth certificate already and just needed the long form. The only potential options provided by New York was to have the name legally changed to show the history of both variations with signed affidavit that they were one and the same person or locate other legal documents showing the variation. A Signature/Name Affidavit from my grandmother stating she was one and the same person and sometimes goes by each variation of her name was not enough. The legal court process for a name change is costly and varies by what county you live in but can be upward of $400. This is an example where baptismal certificates and other evidence may have helped.

Last Name Discrepancies

Last name discrepancies are less forgivable than first name discrepancies. It is recommended that you requested correction of records in this instance. Similar to first name discrepancies, these are usually due to Anglicization or incorrect transcriptions when your ancestor only spoke Italian and an English speaker wrote the record.

Translations

The consulate website will outline which documents require translations. Generally, you must have translations for all the American documents on the Italian side you are tracing. You do not need to translate Italian documents into English nor do you need to translate the Certificate of Naturalization, Statement of No Record, any Letters of Exemplification, Apostilles or your Application related forms. The consulate will generally request that you also get translations for the non-Italian line (the line you are not tracing) just in case those documents are needed for name or date discrepancies.

The consulate website will usually list a number of people that are qualified translators if you do not speak Italian or otherwise can not translate them on your own. I've known people who have used bablefish or other online translators with no issue. Or, you can use other online translation services like Rev, which is typically $33 per page, but for some of the lengthier word heavy documents they will charge you extra fees. Because of this, it's best to have them translate all your documents at once instead of piecemeal to reduce the total count of pages. Since the turnaround time is very fast, typically within 24-48 hours, you should not have any concerns waiting until the end to get the translations.

You may find that some of your documents have data that is handwritten and illegible. When submitting these types of documents for translation you will likely need to provide a typed out version of the handwritten pieces for the translator.

Chapter 10: Frequently Asked Questions

1. Do you get your documents back after you submit with your application? No, you must provide originals and you do not get anything back. This is another reason why it's a good idea to order duplicates of all your documents. At the very least, you should make photocopies of all your documents before your appointment so you will have them for your records.

2. What documents do I need to bring to my appointment? Check the consulate website for specific details based on your situation. However, you will want to bring everything you have collected from your research. If there are questions about dates or names, that extra document you obtained that they didn't explicitly ask for may provide the proof they need and save you from having to make another appointment or mail in more proof after the fact. Check the consulate website frequently, including a couple weeks before your appointment, to make sure none of the required paperwork or rules have changed. I will restate this for emphasis because I have experienced the rules on the website changing. Check and re-check the consulate website after you believe you have obtained everything, a few weeks before your appointment and a few days before your appointment. You can never be too prepared.

3. How do I get an Italian passport? Once your citizenship is recognized, you will receive documentation on how to obtain your Italian passport. You will need a U.S. passport before you can obtain your Italian passport. Once I received the letter that my Italian citizenship was recognized, I was able to get same day service for my Italian passport at the Miami consulate.

4. Why does my Italian passport use my maiden name (for females)? In Italy, females use their maiden names and as such your maiden name will appear on your passport. If you have submitted your marriage certificate and it is registered in your Italian commune, you will be able to have your married name also appear on a different page of your passport. This can help in situations where your driver's license or other forms of identification use your married name. You may want to consider having your maiden name added to your driver's license <First Name> <Maiden Name> <Married Name> to also help avoid some confusion when using your Italian passport.

Your married last name can be added to the passport at a later date since it is displayed on a different page of the passport anyway. This is helpful if you are later married or if, like me, they didn't like my marriage certificate in the first round and I had to provide marriage license as further proof via mail after my appointment.

5. Which passport should I use when travelling? You should use your U.S. passport for entering or exiting the United States. You should use your Italian passport for entering Italy and generally any European Union countries. For any other countries, you should determine which offers you the best benefit. For example, is the country friendlier toward one country versus the other? Is it easier to obtain a travel visa from one country versus the other? Which embassy would you prefer to serve you?

As a matter of practice, you should have your passport ready to go at the airport and avoid letting security know you have two passports. Some security folks are more knowledgeable than others and it's best to avoid a potential delay by a security person who may not realize it's legal for you to have both.

6. How much does it cost to obtain dual citizenship? Check the consulate website for up to date details. Up until July 8, 2014, there were no fees due to the consulate to apply but beginning July 8, 2014 they started charging 300 Euros regardless of the outcome of your application. Additionally, you need to prove that you are eligible by birthright, which involves obtaining a significant amount of documentation that will cost money from each state/jurisdiction in which you need to order originals and obtain apostilles. Each county/state has different fees so how much this venture will cost you varies by person and their situation. You may also decide to employ other folks to help you obtain your documentation, which will cost extra money. This is most commonly needed for obtaining your documents from Italy as well as completing the translations. You are not required to obtain an Italian passport after you have your Italian citizenship recognized. Obviously if you plan to travel, you will likely want to get it. In that case, you will need to pay additional fees similar to your U.S. passport. I have included some sample fees in Chapter 2: Things to Consider.

7. If I was previously married do I need to provide copies of my marriage and/or divorce certificate? Yes. One of the questions for your A.I.R.E (Registry of Italian Nationals residing abroad) is whether you are single, married, divorced or widowed. It will also ask if you were previously married. So, the consulate will request that you register all your documentation even if you are re-married.

8. If my ancestor naturalized does that make me ineligible? It depends. If your ancestor formally went through the process to become a citizen of the United States and in that process lost Italian citizenship, then they still passed the citizenship to their children born prior to the naturalization date. Re-review Chapter 4 for specific laws and examples to help clarify this.

It is very important that if you do a search for the naturalization paperwork and you find your ancestor's name that you order the paperwork even if you see that the 'date' is prior to the birth of the dependent in the line you are following. In my case, I was not sure if my great-grandfather had naturalized or not. I did a search online and found naturalization paperwork that appeared to belong to my great-grandfather. It made sense since the census records indicated that he had applied. The date was earlier than my grandfather's birth so all hope was lost and I assumed I was not eligible but I decided to order the paperwork anyway for ancestry purposes. NARA sent me the Petition for Naturalization and as I read the petition which specifies the petitioner's occupation, birthdate, date of arrival in the United States, spouse and children's names, I quickly realized that this petition was not for my great-grandfather at all. It was likely a cousin bearing the same name since the Italians have a tradition of naming the first male after the paternal grandfather and the first female after the paternal grandmother, second son after the maternal

grandfather and second daughter after the maternal grandmother. In this case, it was quite common to have many children with the same name in the same community. This naming convention knowledge will also help you find older records and sometimes identify where a still born or young child death occurred when at first glance it appears the naming convention was not followed.

Not only was the Petition for Naturalization not that of my great-grandfather, but this petitioner's application was denied anyway "on the ground of ignorance of the institutions and government of the United States". You see, because many Italian immigrants did not speak English well, even if they tried to petition for naturalization that could have been denied and their Italian citizenship then remained intact. Probably very disheartening for them at the time, but probably something you are grateful for now if you are trying to gain dual citizenship and that was the only thing standing in your way.

Chapter 11: Other Resources

1. Obtaining date when your ancestor first came to America: http://ellisisland.org/

2. To research data for your ancestors and obtain documentation: http://www.ancestry.com/ or https://www.familysearch.org/

3. VitalChek website for obtaining any U.S. birth, marriage, death or divorce certificates: http://www.vitalchek.com/

4. For translations: http://www.rev.com/translation or http://www.babelfish.com/ or certified translators recommended by your local consulate

5. USCIS for Certificate of Naturalization or certification of nonexistence of a specific record: http://www.uscis.gov/portal/site/uscis

6. National Archives: http://www.nara.gov

7. Italian form letter generator to obtain copies of records in Italy: http://www.circolocalabrese.org/resources/letters/index.asp

8. Process for obtaining apostille in Florida: http://www.doh.state.fl.us/planning_eval/vital_statistics/apostille.htm

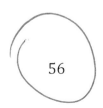

Chapter 12: Reader Q&A

Sometimes more specific questions are helpful to readers than the ones I made extremely generic in Chapter 10 so I've listed some real life questions (slightly altered to avoid giving personal data) below. It's also sometimes helpful to have things answered in a slightly different way or to hear it multiple times so here is an extra chapter in hopes that these scenarios help give you a little clarity on issues you are encountering.

Question 1: My husband's grandfather came to the United States to upstate New York and was naturalized in 1928 (7 years later from arrival). He sent for his wife (husband's grandmother) who came to the United States and 2 years later, had my husband's mother. My husband's mother was 8 years old when her mother naturalized (1944) here in the United States. My husband's mother never renounced her Italian Citizenship (she was born in 1932). My husband was born in 1961. Neither of his great grandparents on either side ever left Italy, they were born and died there as Italian citizens.

Answer 1: Let me see if I have this right.

Your husband was born in 1961 and would be acquiring Italian line from his mother who was born in 1932? That part is okay since he was born after 1948. A female could not pass on the lineage before then. However, we first need to determine if his mother is eligible. I think you are saying her father (she has to get it from her father since she was born before 1948) naturalized in 1928 BEFORE her birth.

In this case, she would not be eligible and therefore your husband is not eligible.

Only question I'd have is how certain you are on the naturalization and date. If he did not sign papers and have them approved (they were not always approved, for example if applicant could not display understanding of English), then he did not relinquish Italian citizenship rights. You should obtain the naturalization paperwork to be sure.

The only way I know of to view the outcome of the Petition is to order the paperwork from NARA. The last section of the Petition has the "Order of the Court Admitting Petitioner" or in cases where the petitioner was denied, they would cross that out and specify that the petitioner was denied along with the reason why.

Question 2: I am trying to obtain Italian citizenship by bloodline (I am a USA citizen) and below is my situation

- My grandfather was born in Italy but became an American citizen in 1925. My father was born in the USA in 1928.
- My grandmother was born in Italy but became an American citizen in 1948 (and was an Italian citizen when my father was born in the USA in 1928).

It seems to me that I will need to follow the line of my grandmother, (since the chain hasn't been broken), It seems that there is some question on whether the blood line can be done with females. I have been on the internet and just can't seem to get any clarity on this.

Answer 2: In your example, since your dad was born in 1928, he wouldn't be able to get citizenship from his mother. However, before you give up all hope...how do you know that your grandfather became an American citizen in 1925? I only ask because sometimes people don't have the actual naturalization paperwork and make assumptions based on when the person came to America, family stories or the date the person applied for citizenship. What matters is when citizenship was obtained and making sure it was after your father's birth. For example, they could have filed a petition one year and not receive a determination for another year or more later which could make a difference. They also could have been denied. You can get a copy of the naturalization paperwork from NARA to be certain.

Question 3: I have viewed all of the documents that make me eligible for jure sanguinis. I am confused how to make the corrections for some of the names. My bisnonno is the relative that naturalized after my grandfather was born. His wife mia bisnonna was born with the name Nunzia Maria <Last Name>. On all her other document she went by Lena <Last Name> (marriage, death, etc.).

Answer 3: Which consulate are you using? Where was your bisnonna born? Where did the marriage of your bisnonna and bisnonno take place? US or Italy?
Since you are applying following the line of your bisnonno, the consulate will ask you to supply

your bisnonna's information but assuming all else is in order they will not place too much importance on your bisnonna's information. Again, this really is at the discretion of the consulate but they will be more concerned about ensuring that the documentation for all the males in your line are in order.

If the documents requiring correction are for events that took place in the United States, then you simply need to follow the directions for correction on the state website tied to the event. For example, if your bisnonno and bisnonna married in New Jersey then you would follow the State of New Jersey correction rules. You would likely just need to supply the birth certificate that would substantiate based on date of birth and parent's names that they are one and the same person and then they will make the correction. If your bisnonna died in Florida, then you would follow the State of Florida correction rules. You would likely need to supply the birth and marriage certificates to show the husband name, dates of birth, etc. to validate the relationships and that they are one and the same.

If you give me more specifics, I can help point you to the correct websites.

Question 4a: I have been unable to find my great-grandmother's marriage certificate anywhere. After my initial appointment with the Newark consulate, I was told that I must find some proof of marriage. This despite the fact that my grandfather's birth certificate clearly has both of my grandparents listed as his parents, with no date or name discrepancies. At my consulate appointment, I even provided various other documents in an effort to substantiate my great-grandparent's marriage. I included copies of certified census records, 2 certified draft cards that have my "great-grandmother" labeled as my great-grandfather's wife, my great-grandmother's AR-2, the certified naturalization declaration and petition for my great grandfather which has her listed as wife, and a certified "record not found" statement from New York city (where they lived their whole lives while in America).

The consulate has currently told me that I must find either a civil or church marriage for my great-grandparents. Given that the marriage occurred in 1907-1908 and my family believes it to have been a church marriage, for all I know these records were lost over the years or even destroyed in a fire or flood. Undaunted, I have dedicated a great deal of time, money, and effort trying to find their actual marriage certificate. Unfortunately this search has so far been to no avail. I imagine I am not the only one who has faced a dilemma like this.

Answer 4a: Regarding your question on the marriage certificate, do you know where they were married? Was it in Italy or the US? I'm guessing Italy. If so, it was fairly common that the marriage took place in the same commune as the birth so that might help in your search. What have you tried so far? What is the full line you are tracing?

Here is a forum I found recently that has some helpful tips. There is a post specifically on what can be accepted in lieu of a marriage certificate. It's important to note that every consulate, and sometimes the person at the consulate, makes determinations that may differ from one consulate person to another so what works for one person sometimes doesn't work for the next. They also like to change the rules sometime. I noticed every time I go out to the Miami consulate website that there is a slight variation on the required documents!

Enough rambling, here is the link:

http://italiancitizenship.freeforums.org/what-was-not-accepted-in-lieu-of-a-marriage-cert-t1404.html

For the most part, they are saying you need the church certificate. If you are looking for an Italian certificate, I can provide details of company I used to obtain mine. I did have to follow-up a number of times and many months went by before I heard anything which is why I did not do a specific call-out in my book for that website, but at the end of the day, they did successfully find the documents I needed and I only had some guesses as to the location and dates in Italy. It looks like they've updated their website a bit and looks like they may have a larger team so hopefully you won't have the same issue. I'd just confirm estimated timing and pricing before you commit to anything.

Hope that helps you. If you answer my questions above, I'll let you know if any other tips or ideas come to mind.

Question 4b: To answer your questions.... I'm tracing and applying through my paternal great-grandfather. I have all his Italian and Brooklyn records save for his marriage record, which should be an American one. Both he and his wife (my great-grandmother) were immigrants to America from Italy.

I really wish it was an Italian marriage certificate I was looking for. Then I would be much more confident I could find it. It's most likely a Brooklyn marriage, and most probably a church one. I've tried everything, and I just can't find it. I am pretty sure that if it was at the city archives, my persistence would eventually have led me to it, but it doesn't seem to be there, so I imagine it was a church marriage. On top of that, it would have been in 1908, the first year that the city required marriage licenses for church weddings, so the license process was not yet being taken that seriously by the churches for another year or two, so many licenses were never returned back to the city.

I've been visiting RC churches around the area they lived, but the worst part about church marriages is that I can't look through the registries myself, which means I have to cross my fingers and hope that the church staffer (usually a volunteer) diligently checks all the possible misspellings and other anomalies that are sometimes rife in records from that early 20th century time period.

I saw that forum post (or similar ones) and came into my consulate appointment with various certified documents which I thought would corroborate marriage, but the consulate still wants a marriage certificate.

Answer 4b: I'm sorry you haven't had any luck finding the marriage certificate. Is that the only document that is holding up the consulate from approving your citizenship? How were you able to narrow down the marriage window to 1907-1908?

The only other option I can think of is to hire a lawyer to review the case if the consulate denies you only on the basis of the marriage certificate. I have heard of cases where a lawyer gets involved (I will check my notes to find the specific scenario one was used successfully) but I think the gist is that you are able to prove that this man is your great-grandfather and the blood chain exists regardless of whether he officially married your great-grandmother so following the rule of jure sanguinis the lack of marriage certificate should not have bearing on your eligibility.

Outcome to Question 4: Actually, I found the marriage certificate late last week. I "rolled the dice", took a road trip and found it in another county's archives where I really wasn't expecting to. Thanks for all your help!

I knew it would be around 1908 based on the 1910 census and also a handful of other documents I had for my great-grandfather, including his passenger manifest which showed his arrival date (1906) and a death certificate after his first son tragically died only after about 10 days. These all helped me to "triangulate" a marriage date.

The next issue/roadblock will probably be that this marriage certificate has tons of discrepancies, and it's more than just misspellings. I think my great-grandfather must have had trouble understanding the English marriage license application at the time, since he had just recently arrived, and even though all his later documents are the ones I have with the LEAST discrepancies, this early marriage certificate I now have is probably the document I have with the MOST discrepancies. Oh well, I'm just glad to have found it.

Question 5: I am starting the document search and gathering process. My family line is this:

Grandfather, born July 8th 1896, came to the US on May 27th 1914 and had 2 children prior to becoming a naturalized citizen of the US. I have his application for naturalization and I am still trying to find the actual signed naturalization papers, but the application to naturalize was made 5 months after my father's birth.

Father - Born April 9th 1923 in the US

I am told I qualify as long as my grandfather did not renounce his citizenship while he was in Italy. I guess it is possible but not very likely that a 15 year old boy who was born in a very poor family in Italy would have known to or had the means to renounce his citizenship in an Italian court. I am not sure what you mean in the paragraph below. Can you elaborate on this and tell me is there is some document I need for this?

Also can you direct me to a place to get all docs including his US and Italian docs in the proper form?

"I brought along all the information from my research including apostilles and translations for the

"non-Italian" bloodline just in case. In the end, they only needed a small portion of what I'd prepared but they also ended up taking some information that I didn't expect them to want, like the census records showing the other children of my ancestor which was also further proof that my ancestor did not naturalize since there is a question in the census to that affect. "

I have a few more questions.

Sometime along his life, my Grandfather changed his first and middle name and used the English version. His birth name if Giuseppe Antonio and that is what is on his naturalization papers. When I looked at a copy of my father's birth certificate it has his father's name written as Joseph Anthony. I am trying to find a name change document but doubt it exists. It is obvious that the name is the same just the English version. His naturalization paper show his child as Joseph with the same birth date as what is on my father's birth certificate and the address on his naturalization papers again is the same address as listed on my father's birth certificate. Do you think this will be an issue and if so how do I correct it?

Also, I was married but I am now divorced. The list of documents on the consulate web site states they want my marriage, divorce and wife's birth certs. Do I just bring my marriage since we are no longer married? Also, they ask for my marriage license. Isn't that the same thing as my marriage certificate?

Answer 5: I agree that it is unlikely your grandfather renounced his citizenship. It is great that you have the application for naturalization so that you have proof it occurred after your father was born and therefore he definitely did not naturalize before then. I don't recall if I mention it in the book but it is possible to be denied when you apply so the naturalization may have never occurred. It's the date naturalization occurred that matters not the application date. Either way sounds like you pass in both cases. Regarding your first question, that paragraph is noting that you should bring along all your research and paperwork because you never know what the consulate may want. Even though they give you a list of documents, they will sometimes want other items that help substantiate. For example, I could not find that my great grandfather ever naturalized. I obtained the proper paperwork requested by the consulate from both the National archives and center of immigration services stating that there was no record. Since there was no record so you are trying to prove something doesn't exists, my consulate also decided they wanted a copy of the 1920 and 1930 census records that I happened to bring along. One of the questions they asked for the census was whether you were alien, had applied for naturalization or had in fact become naturalized. The 1920 record showed that they had applied but the 1930 record showed alien. This means that either the first record was incorrect and they only intending to apply (you have to remember that typically the Italian immigrants did not speak English so many times the children would answer the questions which could cause some discrepancies) or they applied and were denied but either way shows that as of 1930 naturalization did not occur.

The other reason why they may take ancillary info is to show proof that people are one and the same so sometimes tying the other children in the family helps because you can see that a later census file has the same parent names but perhaps your father no longer shows because he was older and moved out but the other siblings from another record are still present. This could help prove either the naturalization question or birthdates, etc.

When I say they didn't take some of my paperwork, it was primarily the "non-Italian" line and many of the translations. If your documentation is strong they generally need less but you should go in with everything to avoid delays.

Besides your grandfather's docs from Italy, it sounds like all your other paperwork are US docs. You can order most of them, if not all, on VitalChek website, there should be a URL in the book. I suggest checking out the apostille rules first though as some docs are easier to order from the state website instead (though I found most were cheaper and more easily found on VitalChek that wasn't always the case, Florida being a good exception).

There, of course, are people that are willing to obtain the docs for you for a fee. However, you should be able to easily obtain all the US docs on you own and just request the long form. All state applications have a spot to specify this even though they may refer to it slightly differently.

Regarding name change, this was very common and depending on who you get at the consulate will determine how forgiving they are on the name change. You should apply for amendment. Every state has a form for correction. Find the state vital records website and you can download the form. You will need proof which will be the birth record or the like with the Italian name to show age and birthdates are the same. The physical record won't be changed but an extra piece of paper will be added to the original document you are amending showing what it should have said instead. This will meet the criteria the consulate needs. Just make sure you get the amendment/correction before you request the apostille and get the translation since the document number will change.

Regarding your divorce, they will want the marriage and divorce records especially if you are trying to get any children from that marriage dual citizenship. If you don't have children from that marriage, they will likely forgive you if you don't have the documents but they will tell you to mail them in later for their records. This is because those docs are not necessary to prove YOUR citizenship so should not impact your application. However, as an Italian citizen they do need copies of all your vital records.

The reason for marriage license and marriage certificate is because many states have limited information on the actual certificate and lots more data on the license. For example, the certificate may just have the bride and groom names, date of wedding and witness whereas the license has your birthdates, parents names and your addresses. The license doesn't prove that a marriage followed so they request both so they can further prove one and the same with all the other detailed information that the license provides.

Hope that helps you. Let me know if you have any other questions.

Question 6: I requested long form documents from Italy. They had that option in the web site. How do I get apostille? What do you mean by apostille rules? I am not sure what apostille is.

For the US docs

Should I pull the 1920 census and just bring it with me? If so who do I get that in long form? Do I apostille this one?

I pull the state birth, death, marriage for each parent, grandparent, and child, the naturalization papers for my grandfather all in long form.

I take all of the docs that need an amendment for name change from Joseph Anthony to Giuseppe Antonio, which is my grandfather's marriage and death certificate and my father's birth certificate and have them amended. Is this a difficult thing to do?

Take the amended documents and have them apostilled (not sure if that word exists)

Take the apostille docs to a translator that is recommended on the consulate website and have them translated.

Ready for the appointment?

A funny story about my grandfather and how he got married. The story my uncle told me was he came to the US in 1914 through NY, which there is no US record showing his entry, went to Pittston PA where I think he had some family. He then moved to Baltimore for work and met my grandmother, fell in love and ran off with her back to Pittston and got married. When he came back, my great grandmother had him arrested for kidnapping (I think she was only 16). The charges were dropped and they lived in Baltimore until they died.

With that being said I tried to request Maryland docs for him and I can't on any website. The VitalChek site said I had to acknowledge and prove I was either him, his wife, child, or court appointed guardian, and so did the archive site for Maryland. They don't answer the phone either. I have filled out all of the mail in forms and was going to attach a letter stating who I was with a copy of my DL, birth cert, and my father's birth cert. that shows I am his grandson.

I also need to get hi marriage license from PA and that's another state that is not available on the VitalChek. I am not sure how hard this will be. I am not sure what name he used and the date of marriage. I only have a date range. Will the state help me get this?

I forgot to ask. How do I get the 1920 census record and get it in long form with Apostille? I found the 1930 federal census with my grandfather's name and the names of my father, uncle and aunts onAncestry.com and it lists him as naturalized but I can't find the 1920 census. How do I locate it?

Answer 6: Let me try to tackle each of your questions one by one.

1. Census records - You should be able to get both the 1920 and 1930 census record from Ancestry.com. Simply print it from your browser. You do NOT need this in any special form or need to order it from anywhere. You do NOT need to get an apostille for it or have it translated either. This is more of a research tool for you but like I mentioned the consulate took it from me as proof in time of "Alien" to further substantiate that there was no record of naturalization.

2. Finding the Census record - You mentioned not being able to find the 1920 census record. Names were often misspelled so you will want to try many variations. I have also found that sometimes the person transcribing the names for the electronic search often mistypes the names because the handwriting is difficult to read even if the census taker wrote it down correctly. So, it is sometimes a hunt to try and find it. There are a number of tricks that Ancestry shares with using only a few letters of the name or if you know where they lived or neighbors they had, tracking them down that way. Remember that the census is not a required document to gain your citizenship so I wouldn't sweat it if everything else is in order but if you can track it down it usually provides some interesting information.

3. Long forms from Italy - What website did you use to request the long forms from Italy? As a reminder, you do NOT need to have ANY records FROM ITALY translated to English nor do you need an apostille for them. Although, if you don't speak Italian you may want to have them translated for your own benefit. The consulate will take the original so make sure you make yourself a copy.

4. What is an apostille? - Apostille is an extra piece of paper from US government that simply certifies that the record is true and accurate and references the Hague convention for purposes of the non-US country to accept that as the authentication of an official record. This is why you must specify which country you need the apostille for because the apostille will make reference to the specific country, i.e. Italy. You need to get the apostille for ALL of your U.S. birth, marriage, death and divorce records. The apostille does NOT need to be translated.

5. Amendments - Amendments are generally not difficult if you have the right documentation. I've found that if the person on the record which you are amending is deceased it is more easily done than if they are living. You will need to fill out an amendment/correction form supplied by the state/county of which you got the record and sufficient evidence of the correct name. For example, if you are trying to correct a marriage record to show that the groom's name matches the name on his birth record, you will need to supply the birth record that shows the correct spelling of the name. The person approving the correction will need proof that they are one in the same which can often be done with just the

birth certificate so long as the parent's names and birth date also line up with the marriage record. However, they will often want you to show proof of your relationship to the person's record you are trying to correct so you will need to show your birth record (if the person is your parent) or possibly multiple records tracing down to you (if say the person is your grandparent). This is most easily done in person but can also be done via mail or online by mailing in copies of all the proof or uploading to a website. Again, each state has slightly different forms and ways to do this. If you are having trouble with a particular one let me know and I can try to help hunt it down for you.

6. Requesting an Apostille - Most states will require you to mail in the original record that requires the apostille so you will be without your original for a short period of time. They will then mail it back to you often with the apostille stapled to the front of the birth, marriage or death certificate. Each state has a different process for requesting an apostille and I even found a state that would let you just fax a copy of the record and then they would mail you the apostille on your own. But for the most part, each state required that you mail in the original. For that reason, you want to request these early in the event anything gets lost in the mail, etc. Unlikely but always a possibility. Also, it is worth noting that because you do NOT need to have the apostille translated, you could have the document translated at the same time you are awaiting the apostille. Most translators will translate from an image you can email them so you don't need to part with any of your originals to get

your required translations.

7. Maryland records - Is your father or grandfather still living? If your father is still living, I'd try to request under his name. It's easiest when you are closest in relation to the record. However, if none of them are still living then you should still be able to get it using the method you mentioned with Driver's License and all the proceeding birth and marriage records to show your lineage to your grandfather. I wasn't sure which record you needed from here (just death?) but here is the website:

http://dhmh.maryland.gov/vsa/SitePages/Home.aspx

8. Pennsylvania Marriage License - Did the consulate say you needed the license too? You often only need the marriage certificate. It's only when the certificate is lacking detailed information that they require the license. Regardless, you should be able to call the county for the record and find out the procedure for getting the license. Just make sure they are clear that you want a copy of the license because most folks want the marriage certificate itself and they don't often get requests for the license so you should describe why you need it and make sure the distinction is clear so you get what you need. This website should help:
http://www.portal.state.pa.us/portal/server.pt/community/marriage_and_divorce_certificates/14126

9. Marriage date - You might want to start with Ancestry.com to try and locate the marriage record with your date range. It's easier to order the

marriage certificate when you have all the relevant info. Pennsylvania keeps the records with the local courthouse so you'd at least need to know which county in PA before you try to solicit their help OR you could have each of them search for you but there may be fees involved.

I think I hit on all your questions. Hope that helps you.

Question 7: I have found all US documents for both father and grandfather except my grandfather's marriage record and have made a request for them. The one record I can't find is my grandfather's marriage certificate. I was told the story of his marriage and where so I requested a search for both names. I hope the story is true and the record is there. If not I am not sure what to do. I have spent about 160 hours searching all of the genealogy sites and the national archives for both Maryland and Pennsylvania and it's coming up with nothing on the marriage certificate. I could only find the 1930 census. I found other people with my last name but not my grandfather. I have not tried to use just the first few letters so I will try that but if I can't find it on Ancestry

Both my father and grandfather are deceased. My mom is still alive.

Once I have the US docs I need to amend 4 different docs.

Grandfather's marriage - assuming the name on it is Joseph

Grandfather's death

Father's birth - only for his father's name

Father's death - again it states his father is Joseph not Giuseppe

After the amendment I send them in parallel to get the apostille and the second set translated. I ordered 2 copies of everything. I found many places on the Internet that have Apostille services. Does this matter? Can I send in all US docs to the same place for this?

When the request for amendment is sent in is the document amended and a record of the amendment kept on file so that all future requests have the amended name or is this just an amendment to a single document? I guess I am asking if I need to send in both copies for amendment.

Answer 7: You want to get the apostille from the state in which the record is from. For example, if you have 3 docs from Maryland send all 3 in at the same time to Maryland. This will save you in some postage fees both ways. I would not use a random website for all the apostilles. Those are companies that will provide it as a service and charge you more for convenience. You'd also want to make sure they are reputable. It's not difficult to do on your own by going to each state's official website.

The amendment is permanent so future requests for a copy of the record or future amendments will show the history of your amendment. Remember that it doesn't change the original record but adds an extra sheet of paper noting the correction.

Chapter 13: Why I obtained dual citizenship

Here are just a few stories shared of why folks obtained their dual citizenship.

"What motivated me to pursue my citizenship is that as a Leadership/OD Consultant, I would really like to work with global companies. I love learning about new cultures and even teach a course at the University on cultural competence and doing business in cross-cultural settings. I am working with a fashion school in Florence, Italy to help them create study abroad opportunities for US and Canadian schools. This has been a very interesting learning experience. Working in Italy as a dual citizen has had two benefits. The first is as soon as I told my client in Florence I was a dual citizen, they were very pleased because they did not feel as though they were taking a job opportunity away from an Italian citizen. The other is that it will make developing a satellite office of my business much easier (if I choose to do this someday)."

"It started off as a connection back to family. After investigating too see if you could hold both I went for it.

I'm also in wait mode on a govt job. On application for security clearance it asks if you have dual citizenship. I don't see it affecting that.

An advantage is easier to travel in EU on the Italian passport. Also obviously easier to work and buy property. Which probably I'd go for in the future.

Health care and retirement options I haven't investigated too much.

Both provided if you decided to work, live, retire there. Would be easy to access. What I have investigated on the health care is typically for better service you have private insurance with the socialized part. I think most good size employers probably offer it private insurance.

I probably will at some point retire there. "

"*I am a college student in Technical Writing and we want to live in Europe, it is our dream. I am going to get my MA degree, but thought it would be beneficial for my children for college if they could have dual citizenship."*

"*I would like dual for ease of travel in Europe, but mostly to be closer to a heritage that I have always considered "my true lineage." I was raised **very** Roman Catholic. Even though my father was of many different descents we lived and breathed Italian culture in my house and in family events. All traditions that we followed were Italian, as if, "everybody did life this way." As a child that is truly what I believed. There really was no outside influence. Not to say we didn't have friends and neighbors of other nationalities, but it never occurred to me that other homes/families ran their lives any differently. I remember telling people when I was little that my mother was 1 of 8 and I was 1 of 5 and that all my aunts and uncles had at least 6 kids too. They would tell me those were big families. I had NO frame of reference; "What do they mean... they are* *big families? Doesn't everybody have that many kids? How else will they have 6 bridesmaids and 6 junior bridesmaids in their weddings, when they only have ONE cousin!? Wow, when they rent out the hall for Christmas parties; they must have a LOT of extra room for dancing" Anyway, I just love Italian culture and I want to recognize it this way and my children to be a part of it . So I want to see what I can do to make it a reality."*

"For me it was pride of my Italian heritage. I am genetically an Italian but culturally an Italo-American and it saddens me on my frequent visits to Italy to seen as "uno straniero". I am a student of Italian history, I have developed a high fluency in the Italian language and obtaining my citizenship was an additional step in moving closer to my ethnic roots. There are potential benefits of being able to work in the EU and of not needing a visa for extended stays in Italia but ultimately obtaining my citizenship was something I did for emotional rather than logical reasons."

Directory of Consulates:

BOSTON (MASSACHUSETTS) - General Consulate
General Consul Liborio Stellino
Address: 600, Atlantic Avenue Boston, MA 02210-2206
Tel: 001 617 7229201, 7229202, 7229203
Fax: 7229407
Homepage: www.consboston.esteri.it
E-mail: archivio.boston@esteri.it

CHICAGO (ILLINOIS) - General Consulate
General Consul Eugenio Sgrò
Address: 500, North Michigan Avenue - Suite 1850 - Chicago, IL 60611
Tel: 001312 4671550/1/2/3
Fax: 4671335
Homepage: www.conschicago.esteri.it
E-mail: italcons.chicago@esteri.it

DETROIT (MICHIGAN) - First Class Consulate
Consul Carlo Romeo
Address: 535 Griswold, Buhl Building Suite 1840 - Detroit, Michigan 48226.
Tel: 001313 9638560
Fax: 9638180
Homepage: http://www.consdetroit.esteri.it/Consolato_Detroit
E-mail: inform.detroit@esteri.it

HOUSTON (TEXAS) - General Consulate
General Consul Cristiano Maggipinto
Address: 1300, Post Oak Boulevard, Suite 660 -
Houston, TX 77056
Tel: 001713 8507520
Fax: 8509113
Homepage: http://www.conshouston.esteri.it/Consol
ato_Houston
E-mail: italcons.houston@esteri.it

LOS ANGELES (CALIFORNIA) - General Consulate
General Consul Diego Brasioli
Address: 12400, Wilshire Blvd., Suite 300 - Los
Angeles, CA 90025
Tel: 001310 8266207, 8263832, 8200622
Fax: 8200727
Homepage: sedi.esteri.it/losangeles
E-mail: la.italcons@itwash.org

MIAMI (FLORIDA) - General Consulate
General Consul Gianfranco Colognato
Address: 4000 Ponce de Leon Blvd, suite 590 - Coral
Gables, FL 33146
Tel: 001305 3746322
Fax: 3747945
Homepage: www.consmiami.esteri.it
E-mail: italianconsulate.miami@esteri.it

NEWARK
One Gateway Center - Suite 100
Newark, NJ 07102
Tel: (973) 643-1448
Fax: (973) 643-3043
Homepage:
http://www.consnewark.esteri.it/Consolato_Newark
E-mail: consolato.newark@esteri.it

NEW YORK - First Class General Consulate
General Consul Antonio Bandini
Address: 690, Park Avenue - New York, NY 10021
Tel: 212 7379100 (int.0)
Fax: 2494945
Homepage: http://www.consnewyork.esteri.it/Consolato_NewYork
E-mail: info.newyork@esteri.it

PHILADELPHIA (PENNSYLVANIA) - General Consulate
General Consul Stefano Mistretta
Address: 1026, Public Ledger Bldg. - 150 South
Independence Mall West Suite 1026 - Philadelphia, PA
19106 - 3470
Tel: 001215 5927329
Fax: 5929808
Homepage: http://www.consfiladelfia.esteri.it/Consolato_Filadelfia
E-mail: urp.filadelfia@esteri.it

SAN FRANCISCO (CALIFORNIA) - General Consulate
General Consul Roberto Falaschi
Address: 2590, Webster Street - San Francisco, CA
94115
Tel: 001415 9314924/5/6
Fax: 9317205
Homepage: www.italcons-sf.org
E-mail: sf.italcons@itwash.org

WASHINGTON D.C. - Embassy of Italy
Ambassador Giovanni Castellaneta
Address: 3000 Whitehaven Street, NW Washington DC
20008
Tel: 001202 612-4400
Fax: 518-2154
Homepage: www.ambwashingtondc.esteri.it
E-mail: stampa.washington@esteri.it

Sample Letters

Requesting an Affidavit of Application for Marriage License from Clark County (Las Vegas marriages)

You should always validate the address and fee as these things may change over time but this will provide you with some sample language of things to include in your request.

Date: <Date>

Marriage Services
PO Box 551603
Las Vegas, NV 89155-1603

To Whom It May Concern:

Enclosed, please find a <money order/cashier's check> in the amount of <Insert amount> made payable to County Clerk for <number> certified copies ($7 each) of my Affidavit of Application for Marriage License. The marriage license is for <Groom Name> and <Bride Name> and was obtained in <Month Year>. I am specifically requesting the Affidavit of Application for Marriage License and not the Certificate of Marriage.

Please mail the <number> certified copies to my home address at: <your home address>.

Sincerely,

<Your Name>

Email to NARA to acquire Statement of No Record

Hello,

I'm in the process of applying for dual citizenship and need to obtain the naturalization records or Statement of No Record for my <relationship>, <Name of Ancestor>. I'm requesting your help in researching whether a record is found.

Here is the information that I have for <Name of Ancestor>.

Person's name (with alternate spellings) - <First Name Last Name>, Alternate first names: <Alternate example 1>, <Alternate Example 2>. Alternate Last name: <Alternate example 1><Alternate Example 2>.

Date and place of birth - <Month Day, Year> in <Location>

Name of spouse & children (if any) - <First and Last Name of Spouse> (<wife/husband>), <First name of child, if applicable> (<son/daughter> <Year of birth – Year of death, if applicable>), <Repeat as necessary for all children>

Approximate year of arrival - <Year>

Place of residence when naturalized (city, county, etc.) - <If you don't believe your ancestor naturalized, this is where you would list that along with details from census files. > <Example: I don't think he naturalized. According to the 1920 Census file, he was living in Lodi, Bergen County, New Jersey

with naturalization status of "PA" (first papers). According to the 1930 census file (still living in Lodi, Bergen County, New Jersey) he was listed with naturalization status of AL (alien). >

Approximate date of naturalization - <Date or N/A with description if you believe ancestor did not naturalize>

If a minor child, the parents' names - <Parent's names or N/A if not a minor child>

Please let me know if you need any other information for your research. Thank you!

<Your Name>

Letter for your packet of information to submit to your consulate/Italian commune

I found a similar letter on the internet and used it to document everything I was including in my submission. Ultimately, the consulate was not interested in the letter or even half of the documents I brought to my appointment. The bloodline documents were solid enough that they did not need the documents from the other side of the family and they really only required the translation of my birth and marriage records. If my mother applied at the same time, they would have needed the translations of all her documents too. However, having this letter was a big help because I labeled the documents in my packet according to the numbers in my letter which made it much easier to find each document as the consulate requested it. It also served as a checklist to make sure I had all the required documents before I left for my appointment.

If you want to go overboard you can also color code your documents with labels.

Obviously, your list will be slightly different than mine but this will give you a starting point of types of things to include in your packet.

<Your Name and Address>

Date: <List date of your appointment since this is when you will be submitting the documents.>

Please accept this completed packet of documents and affidavits. All have been properly notarized, translated and affixed with apostilles.

The binder is labeled with the corresponding numbers to the documents below. Blue tabs indicate documents related to the bloodline I'm following. Yellow tabs indicate marriage certificates (combination Italian line and "non-Italian" line. Red tabs indicate documents related to the "non-Italian" line.

1. Certificate of Birth - <Name of the ancestor born in Italy whose bloodline you are following>
a. Italian copy of record
b. Translation of record to English <This is not required but if you have it, you should include>

2. Certificate of Birth - <Name of the spouse of the ancestor whose bloodline you are following>
a. Italian copy of record
b. Translation of record to English <This is not required but if you have it, you should include>

3. Certificate of Marriage - <Names of the two ancestors above>

4. Statement of No Record related to Naturalization
a. Statement of No Record from the National Archives and Records Administration
b. Statement of No Record from the U.S. Citizenship and Immigration Services

5. Certificate of Birth - <Name of Grandparent for the bloodline you are following, assuming 1 and 2 above were your great-grandparents. Otherwise this is the next person in your bloodline. Skip down or add in more items if you are starting higher or lower than your great-grandparent.>
a. NYC certified copy of record <this sample assumes NYC to show the additional letter of exemplification required>
b. NYC letter of exemplification
c. Apostille
d. Translation of record to Italian

6. Certificate of Birth - <Name of Grandparent, not the bloodline you are following>
a. NYC certified copy of record
b. Translation of record to Italian

7. Certificate of Marriage - <Names of Grandparents for the bloodline you are following>
a. <Abbreviation of State, i.e. NJ> certified copy of record
b. Apostille
c. Translation of record to Italian

8. Certificate of Birth - <Name of Parent, bloodline you are following>
a. <Abbreviation of State, i.e. NJ> certified copy of record
b. Apostille
c. Translation of record to Italian

9. Certificate of Birth - <Name of Parent, not the bloodline you are following>
a. <Abbreviation of State, i.e. NJ> certified copy of record
b. Apostille

10. Certificate of Marriage - <Names of Your Parents>
a. <Abbreviation of State, i.e. NJ> certified copy of record
b. Apostille
c. Translation of record to Italian

11. Certificate of Birth - <Your Name>
a. <Abbreviation of State, i.e. NJ> certified copy of record
b. Apostille
c. Translation of record to Italian

12. Certificate of Marriage - <Your Name & Your Spouse's Name>
a. <Abbreviation of State, i.e. NJ> certified copy of record
b. Apostille
c. Translation of record to Italian

13. Certificate of Birth - <Name of Spouse>
a. <Abbreviation of State, i.e. NJ> certified copy of record
b. Apostille

14. Certificate of Death - <Name of deceased person in the bloodline you are following>
a. <Abbreviation of State, i.e. NJ> certified copy of record
b. Apostille
c. Translation of record to Italian

15. Certificate of Death - <Name of deceased person in the bloodline you are following>
a. <Abbreviation of State, i.e. NJ> certified copy of record
b. Apostille
c. Translation of record to Italian

16. Application for Italian Citizenship Jure Sanguinis - <Your Name>

17. Declaration of Applicant - <Your Name>

18. Declaration of Living Italian Ascendant - <Living ancestor name #1(Anyone alive in the bloodline you are following will need to complete this, repeat this for multiple living ancestors in the Italian bloodline you are following)>

19. Declaration of Deceased Italian Ascendant - <Deceased ancestor name #1 (You will need to complete this for anyone deceased in the bloodline you are following, repeat this for multiple deceased ancestors in the Italian bloodline you are following)>

I would like to register my civil status documents in the commune of my Italian ancestor:

<List commune name and address here. You can obtain it via an internet search.>

Thank you for your prompt attention to my application.

Sincerely,

<Your Name>

Requesting an Apostille

As previously noted, since many states require that you provide a self-addressed, stamped envelope to receive back your apostille(s) it is generally cheaper to try and order all documents from the same state at the same time.

You must list the name of the country in which you need the apostille and it is recommended to list the reason why.

Here is a sample letter to send to each state.

To Whom It May Concern:

I have enclosed the <Name of Vital Record> for <Name listed on Vital Record>. I am requesting an apostille for this document for the country of Italy as part of my dual citizenship application.

I have enclosed a check of <amount of check> per certificate to cover the apostille fees. Please return back to me utilizing the self-addressed, stamped envelope(s) included.

Thank you for your time. You may reach me at the phone number below with any questions.

<Your Name>

\<Your Address\>
\<Your Phone Number\>

Toolkit

Status Spreadsheet

Create a spreadsheet with the following column headings: #, Document Name, For Whom, Obtained?, Apostille?, Translation?, Correction Needed?, Status, Timing, Record Holder State.

#	Doc	For Whom	Obtained?	Apostille?	Translation?	Corrections?	Status	Timing	Record Holder State

\# - To capture each line item and total number of documents needed.

Document Name – To capture the name of the document. For example, birth certificate.

For Whom – To capture the record owner of the document you are requesting. In the case of marriage certificates, there will be two names listed.

Obtained? – Yes and No are valid values. This column is used to track whether you have obtained the document yet or not.

Apostille? – Yes, No and N/A are valid values. This column is used to track whether an apostille is required and whether you have yet received it. You must obtain an apostille for all documents on the "Italian" side that you are tracing. You do not need an apostille for the Certificate of Naturalization or Statement of No Record.

Translation? - Yes, No and N/A are valid values. This column is used to track whether a translation is required and whether you have yet received it.

Correction Needed? – Yes and No are valid values. This column is used to track whether you need to make a correction to the record.

Status – This column can be used to capture when you requested the document or any other pertinent data you want to keep track of.

Timing – The timing of when you plan to obtain. This is helpful if you want to focus on one set of documents per month.

Record Holder State – This is the state in which the event (birth, marriage, death) took place. By doing a sort on this field, you will be able to request records from the same place at that same time to save on fees.

Historical Timeline and List of Discrepancies

A nice addition to your packet of documents is a detailed timeline account of each of the ancestors in your bloodline. I put mine in PowerPoint format. While the consulate ultimately did not want my entire PowerPoint document they did take a few pages from it to help substantiate a few of the documents I had. It also helped tie back nicely to some of the census records since it showed the names of my ancestor's siblings. This helps substantiate that the family is indeed the one connected to your ancestor when the names of children tie to 1920 and 1930 census files or number of births listed on a birth certificate.

This is also a nice way to keep track of all the information you have gathered while obtaining your documents and another checklist to make sure the names and dates match. Now that you've likely become the family historian, you can also share this with the rest of your family as a nice memento.

Generally, I tried to include major life events and specifically ones that I had documentation to substantiate. For example, birth, marriage, divorce, death, dates children were born, dates family moved to alternate locations, graduation dates, schools attended and date of arrival in America.

I labeled the PowerPoint as follows:

<Last Name of Ancestor Following>
Dual Citizenship Application

Then I had slides labeled with the title as the name of the ancestor in the bloodline I was following with the following bullet points:

- Born <Date of Birth> to <Names of Parents> in <Location of Birth> (<Document where this information was validated, e.g. Birth Certificate>)

- Married <Date of Marriage> (age <list age at time of marriage>) to <Name of Spouse> (age <age of spouse at time of marriage>) in <Location of Marriage> (<Document where this information was validated, e.g. Marriage Certificate>)

- Welcomed first child <date of birth or year if actual date is unknown>, <name of first born child>, born in <location of birth> (age <age of ancestor at time of birth>)

- <List any other children born before arrival in America>

- Arrived in America (<location of arrival, e.g. New York, NY>) on <Date of Arrival, Ship if you know the name> (age <age of ancestor at time of arrival>)

- <Son/Daughter>, <Name of child>, is born on <date of birth> in <location of birth> (age <age of ancestor at time of birth>)

- <List any other children before after arrival in America

- Moved to <location> <date or date range> (<name of record where information was validated, e.g. 1920 census file>)

- <List any other children born after date of move listed above>

- Death <if applicable> <Date of Death> in <Location of Death> (age <age at time of death>)

- <Name of ancestor> is buried <Location of burial.> <Any other pertinent data, e.g. name of cemetery, address, name on tombstone, section of cemetery where ancestor is buried, who ancestor is buried with, etc.>

- <You can also include any other relevant details about your ancestor, dates of jobs, etc.>

Agostino Esposito

- Born 15 Feb 1869 to Leonardo and Francesca in Vallelunga Pratameno, Caltanisetta, Sicilia, Italy (Birth Certificate)
- Married 10 Apr 1895 (age 26) to Rosaria Russo (age 17) in Vallelunga Pratameno, Caltanissetta, Sicilia, Italy (Marriage Certificate)
- Welcomed first child in 1898, Rosa, born in Italy (age 29)
- Arrived in America (New York, NY) on 18 Oct 1899 (age 30)

Agostino Esposito

- Son, Leonardo, is born on 31 May 1903 in New York City, NY, USA (age 34)
- Son, Gaetano, is born on 25 June 1906 in New York City, NY, USA (age 37)
- Son, Antonio, is born on 31 May 1908 in New York City, NY, USA (age 39)
- Son, Salvatore, is born on 25 Nov 1910 in New York City, NY, USA (age 41)
- Son, Carmine, is born on 12 Mar 1913 in New York City, NY, USA (age 44)
- Son, Pietro, is born on 17 Jun 1915 in New York City, NY, USA (age 46)

Agostino Esposito

- Son, Giuseppe, is born on 2 Feb 1918 in New York Cit
  NY, USA (age 49)
- Moved to Lodi, New Jersey, USA sometime between
  1918 and 1920 (1920 Census File)
- Daughter, Lucia, is born on 15 Dec 1925 in New Jersey
  USA (age 56)
- Death 22 May 1935 in Lodi, Bergen County, NJ, USA
  (age 66) (Death Certificate)

For each ancestor I also include a slide labeled "<Name of Ancestor> –Discrepancies". For this I only listed the 2 to 3 key documents, depending on whether the person is living or deceased and added a notation about whether or not it was a match.

Example:

- Birth Certificate - <Name as written on Birth Certificate>

- Marriage Certificate - <Name as written on Marriage Certificate (same)

- Death Certificate - <Name as written on Death Certificate> (amendment for correction to name spelling has been placed)

- Birth Certificate – Date of birth <Date of birth on Birth Certificate>

- Marriage Certificate – Date of birth <Date of birth as written on Marriage Certificate (same)

- Death Certificate – Date of birth <Date of birth as written on Death Certificate> (same)

- No date discrepancies!

Agostino Esposito – Discrepancies

- Birth Certificate – Agostino Esposito
- Marriage Certificate – Agostino Esposito (same)
- Death Certificate – Augustino Espasito (amendment for correction to first and last name spelling has been placed)

- Birth Certificate – Date of Birth listed as 15 Feb 1869
- Death Certificate – Date of Birth listed as 30 Aug 1872 (amendment for correction to date of birth has been placed)

Terms and Definitions

Apostille – An apostille is similar to when you get something notarized, but in this case the notary is the issuing state of the certificate. The physical apostille is an additional piece of paper that is affixed to the birth, marriage or death certificate to certify that the document is real and accurate for the country you specify, in this case Italy.

Jure Sanguinis – Latin for "right of blood" which means your citizenship is not based on where you were born but where your parents are citizens.

Naturalize – For purposes of this book, naturalization is the process where a person becomes a citizen in the United States by living in America for a period of time. When folks immigrated to the United States there was a process by which they could formally request citizenship and renounce their prior citizenship (e.g. Italy) by agreeing to the laws of their new country and pledging allegiance to America. Because many Italians did not learn English, some were not able to properly apply or had their citizenship denied since they did not understand the laws to properly plead allegiance. Over time, by virtue of continuing to live in the United States these folks were truly Americans and passed American citizenship to their offspring. In cases where an application was not completed for American citizenship, you will need to obtain a Statement of No Record in order to confirm that your ancestor did not renounce their Italian citizenship.

91800650R00060

Made in the USA
San Bernardino, CA
25 October 2018